MORNING SONG

Wick Poetry Chapbook Series Three
Maggie Anderson, Editor

Any Kind of Excuse
Nin Andrews

Orphics
Leonard Kress

Just One of Those Things
Sarah Perrier

The Several World
Will Toedtman

Stone for an Eye
Karen Craigo

Primer for Non-Native Speakers
Philip Metres

Animals of Habit
Catherine Pierce

Twenty Questions for Robbie Dunkle
J. Gabriel Scala

Morning Song
Joanne Lehman

Stranger Truths
Maureen Passmore

MORNING SONG

Joanne Lehman

The Kent State University Press
Kent & London

© 2005 by Joanne Lehman
Library of Congress Catalog Card Number 2004026728
ISBN 0-87338-834-8
Manufactured in the United States of America

09 08 07 06 05   5 4 3 2 1

The Wick Poetry Chapbook Series is sponsored by the Stan and Tom Wick
Poetry Center and the Department of English at Kent State University.

Library of Congress Cataloging-in-Publication Data
Lehman, Joanne, 1950–
    Morning song / Joanne Lehman.
        p.   cm.—(Wick poetry chapbook series ; ser. 3, no. 9)
    ISBN 0-87338-834-8 (pbk. : alk. paper) ∞
    I. Title.   II. Series.

PS3612.E3545 M67 2005
811'.6—dc22   2004026728
British Library Cataloging-in-Publication data are available.

For my parents—
    Dad, who whistled his morning song on the
        way to the chicken house,
    and in memory of my mother, whose alto
        sings on inside me

CONTENTS

ACKNOWLEDGMENTS

Thanks to the people who helped me find my voice as a poet, starting with Beth Leslie who inspired me with her own poems and favorite poems of others found in her collection of more than two thousand books of poetry. I'm also indebted to Dan Bourne who introduced me to visiting poets at the College of Wooster; Julia Kasdorf who taught me to value my Mennonite heritage as poetic subject matter; and Carolyne Wright who fueled our friendship with Seattle's coffee and inspired me with her energy. Each of these poets guided me in crafting the poems in this collection. I'm grateful to my family and for my friends at Killbuck Valley Writers Guild for listening to my poems and encouraging me. Finally, I would like to thank Maggie Anderson for selecting my work for publication and for her guidance as I revised and completed this collection.

Some of the poems included here were published in slightly different forms as follows: "Not the Apocrypha" was published in *Artful Dodge*, no. 40–41; "Listen to Your Life" was recognized among Distinguished Writers in *Shining Our Light*, 2002, a publication of the Promoting Recovery by Confronting Stigma project, sponsored by Cleveland State University and PLAN of Northeast Ohio; "Morning Song" was published in *Christian Living (Oct.–Nov. 2001)*; and "Neighbors' Hayfields at Dusk" was published in the premier issue of *Farming Magazine* (Spring 2001) and in *The Mennonite*, October 5, 2004.

I

WAGON HITCHER

I.

I was the wagon hitcher. I raised the tongue
heavy as lead, that you propped on
a field stone to make it
less of a weight. At the right moment
I brought it parallel to the ground
while you putt-putted back. I never
doubted the John Deere wheels—
trusted you like God on the seat, your two feet
on the clutch and brake,
you half-turned to watch,
our bond forged with a satisfying clink
when the pin made the hitch.

Then your callused palm closed around
my little one and you lifted me up to the axle—
your arm hugging me onto the seat
in front of you. And for a few rounds
we two farmers breathed crankcase oil,
grime and sweat, sweet clover and clay
the hum of our harvest.

II.

When you asked for the vise grip,
I brought needle-nosed pliers,
a Phillips screw driver, the wrong size
socket wrench.
The pipe wrench wasn't under the sawhorse where
you said it was. There's no time
for tool school to teach me the mysteries and
where to look for a misplaced crowbar.
Too much goes wrong out here where
a hacksaw hangs till the blade

turns orange in the damp neglect
of a farmer's shop. I'm just the worried
daughter, a poor substitute
for the hired help you need.

III.

How did you fix the broken things—
replace missing mower knives, the sheared pins
and frayed belts? How did we
maintain our distance from the power take off and augers?
Rusty bolts could fly off in your face—
chisel fragments imbed a cornea, welding sparks
ignite loose straw. But we kept our
distance and our wits.
Something kept us out of harm's way,
stopped corn pickers and balers
from eating us.

ANOTHER EVE

I remember Mom out there in the yard
chopping up a garter snake with a hoe and me
in a cotton dress just a bare-footed
pig-tailed kid standing beside the broom bush
that our Dad set on fire in the fall—
like Moses' burning bush.

And Mom, who was she? Another Eve
hacking to bits that devil of a garter snake
rather than be tempted into poetry—
beating the rhythm of her fear
into the uncoiling green music.

Years later I want to reach out
my grown up hand and stop her—
say, "You should meet D. H. Lawrence's snake
with its 'yellow-brown slackness'—
or Wendell Berry's—the leaf-patterned back.
Let me introduce you to Mary Oliver's
'cold cauldron . . . six months below simmer . . .'"

But it's too late to change that day.
I'll never go back to live childhood over.
Here, in this memory, I stand forever in the yard,
mute, helpless, and barefoot—
knowing what I didn't know then;
wishing to life the things I didn't say.

HYDRANGEA

I stayed at my parent's house the day
before Mom's surgery.
At midnight there was a storm—
hard rain and lightning.
I awakened and thought, *This
storm is our life. Here we are, walking into
the storm.*

The prayers had been said
and my mother's forehead still wore
the anointing oil—
I don't want to do this, she kept saying.
My brave words, and our future
were drowned out with the thunder.

Back home, days later, I cut
all the hydrangea
blossoms from the bush she
gave this year for my birthday.
I want to save them and remember
how it was that afternoon—how she smiled
and we sang hymns,
sitting at the dining room table,
her face soft and
beautiful, as we waited
for what would happen next.

TEAR SOUP

I still have grieving to do.
A winter day with
sunshine on the snow
begs me like a hot bowl of soup
to dip into the broth of our loss.
There are so many things I didn't tell you.
It was some insistence by both
of us to keep things simple
between us. Joy was as close
as the table centerpiece, remade
with a sprig of silk ivy.

The mistakes we talked about
were small—a card we should have sent;
a different color; a smaller size.
We wouldn't go further.
You wanted everything nice and we
kept it that way as long as possible.

This morning I tried on your
brown boots. I kept them,
thinking they might do
but when I look down on them
I know they won't.
I remember too well your
feet in them and your small
hesitant steps over the glassed-in
hospital bridge. I could eat
my words this afternoon
if they were in this soup.

I'd swallow back everything
I said that day as I tried to create
courage between us. We
knew nothing would change,

even though I spoke. But
that day you didn't change the subject
to something pleasant.
The only sound after that
was our footsteps taking us down the long corridor.

MAPQUEST

Outside my window this afternoon
a strand of crystal rain pearls strung themselves
along the hydrangea stalk where the heavy blossom
bowed it down. I didn't notice these the year my mother
was dying. Back then—three, four years now—
we lived day to day saying hopeful signs
and giving each other directions.

Take I-271 and get off at Chagrin Boulevard. You will cross
Belvoir and Green Road. Stay on 422 at Fairmount Circle . . . "
We learned to drive to University Hospital.
After the cemetery with the iron fence you come to
Little Italy—colorful street murals on the wall—
We didn't stop to sample pastries or savor a Tuscan dinner.
Whole conversations were about finding a space
in the parking deck, the ticket you get stamped at the desk.

We sat in the cafeteria's false cheer—
foolish fountains and palms of the atrium. We stayed
as long as we dared, watching the gathering scrub nurses,
students cramming for exams, masked green doctors,
Amish and Islam and pale children with no hair who sat under
IV poles strung with red and silver balloons. We ate
and waited, but each time our food became a hard stone.

Today I'm crying with the hydrangea.
I remember how I brought them in a vase to her room,
wishing away the city of Cleveland.
All we did back then was try to find our way,
go the only direction we could, carry flowers
and listen to the steady drip of Nutrimax
as we blanked out all talk of food.

I still lose my way on a day like today—feel the crumpled
map in one hand, a cup of hospital coffee in the other.
At the unfamiliar intersection I still feel lost—
travel-weary—as if I'd slept all night on the window sill
in her hospital room.

THIS RAIN

That painted tin roof, shining.
The grief never goes. Dame's rocket, mistaken
for sweet William,
Some of it we get used to—
the long silences, distance that can't be closed,
the train whistle, a siren that blasts noon,
Westminster chimes on the Old Main clock.

Never the grief . . .
The old elms struck by lightning,
weed-whacked thistles wanting to bloom purple,
moldy hay—caught in love's rain dance,
the cow that had to be put down,
bloated, swarming with flies.

Prayers with the mourning doves don't get you over it—
we still miss that ragged coat
but it had to be burned.
We cry for every whitewashed rock, the green hillside
turned into highway.

Some of it . . .
They say you get used to—sweet sacrifice,
the memory of a single milkweed blossom
offered in the outstretched hand at dusk along the road.
A lone goose, flying north,
Books we should have kept, the ones we never read
I say the heart will never . . .

Feathers stolen from where they dropped,
the unhatchling,
sandstone that didn't fossil, a shady grove
long summer back. Grief never goes the distance.

Hummingbird nectar could feed us
from the shaded porch swing. Now the faded lavender dress,
linen-like, but made of hemp, won't fit.
The grief never goes, its distance can't be closed.

The heaviness of a dark sky at noon, brittle corn,
cut down and gleaned by sandhill crane.
This unwanted ending—blue depths, the eyes
that begged us not to go,
fallen tulip petals, lilac gone brown,
the broken plate we couldn't fix.

I say the heart will never—distances, heavy skies.
This rain. Brown's bog, every fern.
This grief, late spring,
when the wood thrush called my name.

II

POTTERY MUSEUM

At the pottery museum in East Liverpool they have
all the old dishes, bowls, pitchers, soup tureens and platters—
even a green, four-foot china trophy honoring
the fastest-flying carrier pigeon.

Bowls embellished with gold, stamped on the
bottom with trademarks: Homer Laughlin China Company,
or Vodreys, Rockingham. Everyone back then
knew clay and practiced shaping it into a vessel—

copies of European china—the voices these pieces had.
Here they gather on glass shelves—
none holding water or dough or fine ladies' calling cards,
Sunday dinner. A life still, in their emptiness.

Even the equipment used to make them remains—
this old iron vise to flatten a dozen hanging
flaps of clay, squeezing water out, preparing a
soggy, malleable slab. Clay, waiting to become

yellow ware, white ware, Grandma's wedding dishes
crazed with advanced age—gold-glazed rims,
and the lacy, long-extinct fanciful lotus-wear,
a revelation of what all clay might have been.

HYMN SING

It's the old black hymnal
that makes us sing, really sing
and remember the way we grew
dedicated and hoarse.
Having been given all the words
such a long time ago, we still carry
them in our hearts with their tunes.

It's been years, maybe never,
since we harmonized like this—
but now sitting at the table in
the unlikely geography of tonight
we pour hymns out
like wine. We hold
the book between us,
handing it back and forth
to remember and reclaim
our liturgy.

The old, old stories
pour forth with their own notes.
The friend who was once just
a sister carries her part.
Jesus and grace outshine sin
and the breath of God
sighs, returning us to
this place.

We rise from the table
graced and amazed,
clay shaped by the potter.

MORNING SONG

I owe my Lord a morning song. How can I help but sing
when God is all in all, and I am one with ev'rything.

—John Bell

The debt on that morning song
the Mennonites owed the Lord
was paid in full yesterday when
the Scottish songwriter innocently
handed our words back to us and
told us about a God who loves
enough to change. Suddenly
the whole congregation was on its feet
singing the new words in their new tune—
as fresh and crisp as winter air
rushing into the lungs of a soul.

Someone will probably miss the hymn
invented in 1890 by Mennonite farmer
Amos Herr, but not those who rose up
jubilant there. The old familiar tune
is called "Gratitude" though it wasn't until
mid-morning yesterday that we knew
the places our gratitude might take us
or how songs weave themselves into us
and out again when the invocation is
sung in the barn before daylight
while the horses munch their oats
and stomp the beat of our prayers
on the packed clay floor.

Some of us were surprised
how our hungry hearts
reached across the table
to drink the new song like milk—
having droned the old "Gratitude"

day after day over bowls of
Mother's Oats growing cold
in the dark January mornings of childhood,
while the brown sugar melted away
in sweet weepy ooze.

TWIN SPEAKERS

The Detweiler twins—Bill and Bob—
took over the Calvary Hour Broadcast
when their father died.
"Twin Speakers" they liked to say back
in the infancy of stereo. For decades the
Mennonites listened to them on the car
radio on the way to church. The sermon
before the sermon.

Every time the twins were together
they wore matching suits, shirts, and ties—
even after their hair went white and they
lived in separate states with their blonde wives.
Everyone thought how good it was
that they looked identical. You couldn't
tell them apart.

The day before Bob's daughter married,
he died mowing the lawn. Bill put on
the suit Bob bought for him and
performed the wedding ceremony.
(They always gave you a better deal
if you bought two, he told someone later.)
The undertaker dressed Bob in one suit
and Bill wore the other to the funeral,
next day. For months afterward
he wished the note in the breast pocket
had been from Bob, but it only said

Inspected by #00557. One voice
goes on preaching. The message is
still the same: always about what
you choose, who is saved, and what
happens when you die.

NOT THE APOCRYPHA

The Sunday school teachers don't tell
all the stories about Samson—how he
tied the tails of foxes together and
set them on fire to create a whirling
dervish of his own. Not mentioned,
the time he dug wild honey out of a rotting lion
and took it home to his parents
for supper.

They never tell
how God commanded Jeremiah
to bury his underwear and dig it up later
or how David lounged on the palace porch
with binoculars, wearing only a loin cloth,
to watch Bathsheba
sunbathe nude on her roof.

They didn't tell us where to read
about youthful nipples
that look exactly like the faces of
twin deer—a pretty accurate
picture if you'd had any
experience to compare it with.
They didn't want to awaken desire
or have us imagine the curve of a thigh,
breasts heavy as coconuts, the navel
a goblet biblical lovers drank from
in vineyards at midnight.

And no one mentioned how Noah
got smashed and exposed himself
to his family almost as soon as he could
ferment the wild grapes he cultivated
in the wet field just to the northeast
of the ark where they were living at the time.

We were never introduced to Onan, the
rowdy, pig-headed character
who spilled his seed on the ground.

We're not talking agriculture here,
but everything—
streetwalkers who sent men over the wall,
down their red bed sheets to safety,
Goliath's hair entwined
in David's fingers. John the Baptist's
glassy-eyed head on a platter,
and the sensual dance of Salome
who bought it from Herod.

This story is Isaac bound and gagged
with a knife to his throat, saved the
last instant by the ram in the thicket.
We carried in our hearts what the Sunday school
teachers said. They told us the truth—
how the door of history's
improbably hinged on a Father
who watched his son's execution—
as those red-beaked vultures circle.
God placed his only Son's hands on the rack
and waited for death with the rest of us—
walked away rather than look at
those tendons seeping out life
on the rough-hewn timber.

ELI'S BROTHER

Eli and his wife welcome me
to their sitting room.
His steel gray shirt is a fine fabric,
crisply pressed shirt sleeves
shine silver in kerosene light.

Closely set blue eyes pierce
the space between us and his Rocky boots
are new and clean—saved for evening
and his appointments.

If you want to speak with me again,
you should make an appointment, he says.
How you do that when you can't call
on the phone isn't explained.

Eli has a fifty-five-year-old brother locked
in the back room naked—he won't wear clothes.
He's safe. Feels at home. *We feed him.*
No one says his name.

AMISH FRIENDS

Your horses fulsome and great,
with clobbering hooves and their brushy socks—
how you care for them and walk
in your fields, dreaming of alfalfa.
Who'd think I could lust for a
ripe tomato or get high on a glimpse
of your garden—larkspur and cockscomb?

For me, non-essentials take the better part
until I'm weepy. And then, I come here and
look down, see the soil,
with your feet in the furrow.
We talk of tracks and dust. *Need rain.*

Your silo is full, but I'm empty.
You'll probably plow for winter wheat
and sow, never guessing it was envy
that backed away and eased on to the road
heading north, praying for
something simple like rain
or a single waterfowl outstretched
lapping across a red sky later.

TRACKS

What was I so busy doing, I wonder
that I never explored the banks of Sugar Creek
or roamed the woods with you behind
the house? I was sewing a new dress I didn't need,
trying out soybean recipes,
stripping ugly wallpaper,
painting the woodwork
two coats of Old Sturbridge Mustard.

You came home covered with mud
and nettles, cocklebur. I taught you to
leave your shoes on the porch,
demanded clean hands before supper.
I pre-treated the grass-stained knees
of your Wrangler jeans,
stripped yellow wax build-up
from the kitchen floor with ammonia.

Now, this winter evening so many years later
you and your family arrive for a visit.
You stay outside exploring the snowy woods.
I heat up leftover soup, butter bread for grilled cheese.
Tall, in your work boots you finally stand
your ground in my kitchen
Mom, come out to the woods,
I can show you some things . . .

I'm still busy. *But, I'm making sandwiches . . .*

We can make them later. My agenda dismissed
with a wave. My boy guides me to discoveries—
tracks of squirrels, our cat, the neighbor's dog.
Some low-slung animal that left a trough
where his belly dragged.

But the nine deer we saw at Christmas
haven't come back. Here a young buck
rubbed his antlers on a sapling,
here a larger one, a larger tree.

We compare dog tracks with unmistakable coyote prints,
sharp claws etched on wood's edge behind the rabbit tracks
tight and close. In the bramble
you show me signs, a warm body,
melted into the days-old snow—
the wild leap—a snowshoe hare sprung,
hind legs leaving their deep mark,
the front feet a faint print stretching
away from ours, headed home.

MARCH BLIZZARD

For Margaret and David

Late in the afternoon
on the day you leave
I sit and read what you wrote.
Out on the balcony a ripe
March snow lifts
five inches off the railing.
Your poems come as if ripped
from my center and sift back through
to my hollow core where I'm
somebody else—not the one
they all know.

I sit and think
of the room where I don't live—
the way we sat there together noticing
the half-sewed dress on a hanger,
serviceable black shoes.
Life is complicated here,
We can't be what you are.
I am longing for the life I don't have.
Now, the March blizzard suggests my
too short measure, a false acceptance
of yesterday's faded hills
that today's fresh snow flaunts.

Always, when you live where we do
you wonder about the snow;
where to put the part of you that
loves the unsaid; how to make peace

with the gray woods
and when to reach for the door,
its smooth weighted hardware
finally right in your cold hand
as it swings free, open.

III

WELLSVILLE, OHIO

This afternoon I want to go
to a river
and watch the muddy water
ride out winter—
me on the coal barge
inching its way.
Or just standing on River Street.

The stone wall in Wellsville
would contain me
and any old clapboard
house would do for a vantage
to watch this life pass by.
I could stand in the window there
looking out; waiting for nothing
I know as yet impossible.

There, every winter rain
is another drop
in the deep current,
every sunrise a movement to
swell these bare branches,
every droplet a promise—
of one green shoot
on a bare tree.

STILL WINTER

You take me in your field walking
with Sadie, the yellow dog, a black cat.
We go across the stubble pasture.
I'm comfortable in my boots
as with you on the brown
thatch of your dormant hayfield.
We came here so easily.

Now we sink down into the wooded gorge
on a narrow path.
It is mid-winter with mud.
We can only imagine
wild rose, trillium
spring beauty, sweet William.

But there is more to show me—
an old springhouse,
stone walls shifting under its weight.
The cement floor is clean-swept,
across the end artesian water
brims the chill trough.
Once you almost
drowned here, you were so small.

We could be anywhere—
the south of France, Tuscany,
an Ohio prairie homestead. But we are at home.
How comfortably the cellar hinges creak.

The fireplace is tall enough to walk in
and an iron kettle waits above the
bare hearth. Timber walls
filled in with hard-packed
clay are plastered over and whitewashed,
crumbled with age.

Empty crocks and clay jars
rest on the shelves.
Old tools hang under the eaves
a still life we can
return ourselves to—
this feast at the bottom of memory.

LISTEN TO YOUR LIFE

Listen to your life.
It will speak from
empty sidewalks, whispered
droplets on the asphalt
after you've left the singing children
in the school auditorium.

Listen to your life
in the echo
bouncing back to you from the eyes
of the stranger
sitting in the front row.

Listen to your life in the
unnamed dreams rising
in rumpled softness. Pull
your life out of the dry grass
at the edge of November
and carry it on your body
like a bead necklace.

Listen to your life. It is
the silent house, the dark
afternoon when you are still
at your desk, a chance
meeting on a street corner,
the swans on the pond
you passed by yesterday.

RED ONION

The night after I interviewed you
the full moon shone in my window
and kept me awake thinking
and thinking about shadows
and light and the
sphere of reflection.
I wanted one of us to capture
the bare tree branches
holding up the moon with tender arms.

We could name this longing for beauty
and define the piercing insouciance
of a solitary star reaching out
from the hole in the night.
You finger fabric, touching the silk
and satin, clipping and knotting challis
you stitch up comfort out of fear,
with your needle.

You paint hope around a photographed sunset
and take pictures of strawberries on
the windowsill of your apartment
rather than go out.
I heard strength in your voice when you told
me about your friend's beautiful hands.
You stopped cooking to photograph
her holding a red onion—two amazing yellow cores
and a purple globe wrapped in a lettuce leaf,
beauty before dinner.

Now, out here in the country
where the full moon casts shadows
I think of how you told me when you're
alone, just to hear a voice,
you'll call someone after midnight.

COLUMBIANA COUNTY

Carol has a clutch of blacksnake
skins coiled inside a glass gallon pickle jar
on the shelf with Faulkner and her Victorian poets.

She's my age and still mischievous like that.
She cooks on an antique gas stove and lives
with six cats—one who is diabetic.

The field of black-eyed Susans outside her
back door are just black heads
since the frost. We walk past

them on the way to her pick-up. She gives
me a map of the county I left her in a long
time ago. We explore our landscape

all day. A broken bird's egg—a blue heron or wood duck
she thinks—sits on the dashboard of her green Toyota.
And me, in the passenger's seat.

WILD HONEY

Tonight is the end of July.
The crickets, locusts and tree frogs are
singing for all they're worth
out there in the woods.

If you don't have anything to say,
or if you have so much you don't
know where to start,
just listen and still yourself.

The words will flow out of you
when they're ready.
And in the meantime, these others
speak for all creation
in exuberant, erotic,
exotic night song.

Do you hear them?
They are calling out to you
all night, wanting you to listen—
pleading for you to pay attention
their voices loud as the prophet's
who once ate them
sweetened with wild honey
to stay alive.

NEIGHBORS' HAYFIELDS AT DUSK

For you, my neighbors, it may look like disaster—
you waited compassionately

for the young to fledge, but then it rains. The hay cut,
not even wind-rowed yet, and everything soaked,

silvery and pale on the damp ground.
At dusk I walk in the road between your two hayfields

and in the emptiness between one breath and the next
I see a redwing blackbird up on a wire

coach her chick to lift off and fly. In the distance
a whole choir of them rises, winging evensong.

My heart comes to rest with theirs
on the first damp cutting. And how yesterday I ached

to join the barn swallows
as they dipped into the uncut grass, swooping

and lifting, their forked tails dark
against their bellies, blue-black backs

arching toward the vaulted sky, the reservoir
of all that matters. Out here, day after day

my worship is fashioned out of this breath
taken in on the road between your two fields

where everything is damp and rejoicing, waiting
in anticipation for the sun to mount the high altar,

dry hay by the end of the week; fireflies
by the end of the month.